PRAISE FOR
Gravity's Angel: A Collection of Poems by Kevin Ducey

You'll find a metaphysical film festival, a killer jukebox, and a rare books library tucked inside a Kevin Ducey collection, and Gravity's Angel is no exception. Call it a tribute album, call it a people's history of work, war, and the hungers we can and can't name. Wherever she is, Simone Weil is feeling a bit more seen and understood.

— Erin Keane, editor in chief, Salon, and author of *Runaway: Notes on the Myths That Made Me*

GRAVITY'S ANGEL

A COLLECTION OF POEMS BY

KEVIN DUCEY

First published in Great Britain in 2023 by Kingston University Press

Copyright © Kevin Ducey 2023

ISBN 9781909362734

Typeset in Ernestine Pro

Editorial and Design by Kingston University
MA Publishing Students: Susanna Marie Hutto,
Rakshita Pawar, Saida Adila Sukman and Jovana Sretenov.

Kingston University Press
Penrhyn Road,
Kingston-upon-Thames KT1 2EE

TABLE OF CONTENTS

ACKNOWLEDGMENTS

My thanks to the editors of the following journals for publishing the some of the poems included here. Malahat Review, AGNI, Literary Imagination, LVNG, The Notre Dame Review, Dislocate, Beloit Poetry Journal, Crazyhorse, Cannot Exist, Zoland, Antioch Review, Poetry Salzburg Review, and Stand.

Some of these poems were written with the support of a grant from the Wisconsin Arts Board.

i

FOREWORD

Simone Weil was born in Paris and grew up in a secular Jewish family. Her father was a doctor, and her older brother, André, grew up to be one of the century's famous mathematicians. He specialized in topology, studying the mutability and resilience of form. Simone was a scholar of Plato and Marx, a teacher of philosophy and a social activist. André and Simone shared a lifelong interest in Hinduism.

The one book manuscript she completed in her short life, "Oppression and Liberty," critiques both the capitalist and communist misunderstandings of labor. She fought, briefly, in the Spanish Civil War for the Anarchists. Invalided home, she fell under the sway of the poetry of George Herbert and developed an enthusiasm for Christian mysticism.

In 1940, the family fled Paris ahead of the German occupation, first to Vichy then to New York two years later. Simone returned to London to work with De Gaulle's Free French government- in-exile. While in England, she developed plans for the reform of French education and worked toward her dream of leading a legion of French paratroop nurses.

She died in 1943, at age thirty-four, of complications from tuberculosis. Some say it was starvation, though the cause is disputed (her insistence on keeping to the diet dictated by the Nazis for the workers of wartime France probably didn't help her chances for recovery). She was, in any case, as Sontag has told us, sick.

I was drawn to write these short propositions on Simone Weil's life for a number of reasons. From her earliest writings her intent was to demonstrate the practical uses of doubt. The impression the world makes on the self and one's reaction to that impression, she referred to as the "imagination." Her sense of the imagination as something active in the world struck me as more useful than the English Romantic's employment of that word.

Her clarity and directness appealed to me. Her preoccupation was with labor, both as a practical matter and as a manifestation of the imagination. This insistence on labor, on affliction and the work the world makes of us, is perhaps the most eloquent defense of poetry, or the personality, anyone has written. I took it to heart and never looked back.

ONE

*And is it not purification really
that which has been mentioned
so often in our discussion?*
– SOCRATES "PHAEDO"

BEAUTY, FIRST WHALE THEN MONKEY

Starting with a line from Rufus Wainwright

Beauty you make me sad.
If you were a whale
and I a ship, I'd see you
coming for me:

a rocket through the water,
trailing incandescence
like celebrity's entourage.

Tell me again it wasn't about Fay.
My sides have windows
and off the top of my head you saw

the wars of mankind
wrapped in bandages

in such a way that Achilles might weep –
tying the rag ends about the wound

so that beauty might carry me
in her arms like a bit of
David Bowie stage business.

Remember love, how we hate
our television,
all those false exclusions
from a box – where even Helen
once put her hand
on Hector's bloody arm
when he came home.

COIL, SLAB, HELIX

1

"They have some pots
that are simply
impressions of a fist
in mud – not even
coil or slab."

       He
went on in this way.
"Some cultures are
better than others –"
his eyes following his
ex-wife about the room as the
conversation drifted.
          "These were
not Greeks and I'm not
talking about ornament here –"
            she was
dressed in Madras and
sandals. He straightened his tie.
          I caught
in that first crude jug,
punched out of a fist
of Mississippi clay,
an impress of sorts
of the wing'd chariot
swooping down on
Wordsworth in his rowboat:
     How the mountain
     rises up to meet you.

"Though it takes
no great skill to heap
up a lot of dirt. Monk's
Mound no ornamental
                    Palenque.

There's no writing,"
he said. "Even animal skins will
survive into our time, but
there's no writing."
                    She brought
her new boyfriend
                    dogging
her heel. "The Mayans
wrote, sure, but the
connection hasn't
been established yet.
                    It'll come.
One day. There are hundreds
of grad students –"
                    he watches
her over the rim of his wineglass
"working on this. Somebody
help, I mean, somebody'll
make a career on a DNA trace."

2
Who is the ghost returning
returning to the world
that has forgotten him?

Hamlet's father hovers
over the roofline. The
attention wavers and the jungle

treeline will have to be
blown back with napalm. The
father pauses, a wisp
of smoke asking our
remembrance. Asking.
                    Ulysses
pulls his chair away from

the fire. The return to his
house, but in disguise. Rites
of passage: we don't know who

we are. Hovering over the
roofline. Visiting death upon
his birthday – the old nurse

recognizes the scar on his
thigh. Who it is – remembrance. And
he takes her by the throat.

3
Some grad student will
do it – trace a caduceus
twining up the
Mississippi from the
Gulf of Mexico – not love
at all.
        A potter's fist
pressed into a slab of
clay – lifted to one's lips
a trace of dust.
                Sure,
she's brought her
new squeeze. Oh, mercy,

I won't tell; with the house
full of suitors – only one
        dissembler.

4
Before becoming garage
mechanics, they had
hunted egrets, and they
described their technique,
which consisted
in placing cornets
of white paper on
the ground in such a way
that when the tall birds,
fascinated by the
immaculate whiteness
similar to their own,
thrust their beaks
into them, they became
hoods which blinded
the birds and made them
easy to capture.

The finest feathers
were plucked from
living birds during the
mating season. There
were, in Cuiaba,
cupboards full of egret
feathers, since
the noiseless collapse
of the feather market.

5 Ghost stories

Abraham ties the son to stone
lifting ritual blade, bringing
it down to cut
                just a little.
"He lak'd a lyttle," said the Green
Knight.
            A little. They still
meet like this sometimes. For
the sake of the children.
Parties. The boy's eighth-
grade graduation. He comes
laughing through the kitchen.

                The father
grasps love by the throat to keep
his name unspoken. Ulysses,
it could be anyone, or no
one who has blinded us. Hovering
over that roofline blinded
by love, told to be silent.

It could be anyone –
I asked who your friend was
you said: "Santa Claus" or

                "Lev Davidovich"
in Mexico, as he pulls his glasses
from their case, bends
to read the article his daughter's
young man has written.

"The consumption of articles
precedes their production."

Lev laughs, "only in a world
of credit.
            And what
banker would bet on us?"

Ah ha ha, in that last
breath he senses
the mountain
rising up as fast
as we can row –

The potter made the
vessel pressing his
fist into the wet clay, we
manage a DNA trace
to drink. The glasses
tranquil as Mount Popocapetl
on the blotting paper
in Mexico as he bends
to read. Christmas' heavy
boot tread in the hall,
hovering along that winter
horizon with an ice axe.

6
The anthropologist stopped
along his safari to ask
how the egrets were getting on.

Lord how they fly. He traces
tribal face markings on white paper
one thing leading to another:

they're continually making
sense. They can't help it. It
is not a recapitulation.

Take the children
into the bush and
we can't help them.

Child running through
    a kitchen
brought up short at the sight
of his father.

Traced across his
forehead, listing to the
father's complaint – whether
    we will or no –
the helix pulled
from potter's wheel.

WHO'S YOUR FRIEND?

Max Michelson, Imagist poet 1880-1953

The Imagist fades away out of the metro
and into the Seattle mist of 1918. He finds
the soldiers and sailors there
"less patriotic" and speaks with "contempt
of the bugaboo of death." In a year
those soldiers of Seattle were out in the streets –
the red bandana on their arms. An image
thrown against the coming storm. Images all
come with baggage. The lumber barons
were lynching these soldiers
before the decade was out and the
Spanish influenza blew in on the train with
the demobilized. Max was packed off: "rest,
diet, catharsis, hydrotherapy." A time
of plague and Palmer Raids.
                                        Imagine
a country with an unpatriotic military
(there's an image wavering in the
current heat). The Post Office in Chicago
refused to deliver any Union material
and Heywood fled the country.
                                        And Max –
in the Seattle Sanitarium – demanded
a new hearing. "I had nothing to do
with the conspiracy to blow up that
Post Office. It's a dirty story..."
The image is a variety of letter
bomb after all and Max's insistence
on an IWW lawyer reconciled politics
and the imagination better than the rants
on usury sung out of St. Elizabeth's.

BLACKFRIARS

God's banker killed by mafia, experts rule.
THE OBSERVER, DECEMBER 7, 2003

The Banco Ambrosiano goes in black,
the doors shuttered; the
pope's treasurer has gone missing.
The angels carry the man to
Blackfriars Bridge where they leave
him swing.
        They've chartered a boat
and carry God's banker sweating and
pleading to the river – following
the Sex Pistols into the current. God
save the Pope's Bank Manager;
he ain't no financier.
           The angels feign
no interest in your grand feelings.
Their compound eyes never blink.

Movement stills on the crowded street.
The holy silence of the plastic shopping
bag blowing along a gutter. This way
to the river,
        the hierarch's motorcade rushes
past – a pale hand pressed to the limo's glass.

BOTTICELLI'S ANNUNCIATION OF SYNAPSID RELATIVES

– After New York Natural History Museum and the Cloisters

Blue lightning gestation through windows
the archangel reels (a scrim of
architecture seemly between). Five
hundred million years since the first
backbone. Meryl Streep whispers
in angelic voice-over: "the virgin
kneeling – same with messenger –
everybody, kneel." Meryl says: "Diplodócus."

Mammals and our extinct relatives all
with holes in the head. Thus, the messenger
enters via trapdoor in ceiling: a scatter
of gold
        overhead, plaster'd wisdom and
tawdry sly look lingering under her brow.

BROTHER GEOMETRY

André and Simone Weil

I
Your lips blue in anger
a smile tight as your hair
twisted in my hands. Your
fist in
        my face.
Dear brother, how
I love to bring
my foot
     down hard on your
toe, to
    hear you cry out;
                still –

I'd rather have let you win, rather
give in,
     than let them send us
separately to our rooms.

My mother's idiot friend
who pointed us out:
"Genius and Beauty" was
Ugly and Stupid: how
can people speak
before knowing anything? Or,
is it all we will ever do? Tell me again,
the chiasmus of the
quadrilateral – I'm the slightest
angle off-center and never
convinced it'll come straight.

II
Under the kitchen
table your whisper in my
ear. Tracing your
letters as I copy. Words,
numbers, equation,
                    and
balance. Where I stand
on the quay watching you,
my brother, swimming away
in maths. "It's easy," you say. "Here,
again, like this..." The geometrical
road to light: one moves, learns
by angles. Labor in any field
you choose & the trade works
its way into the body.

The news from Shanghai
brings word of famine and the world
hangs suspended in hunger (twins
always bring
                    bad luck). Beauty
and genius – one stick taken up
to beat the other.

THE SUSSEX

I don't want to go to Sumer anymore.

Want to stay in
or wander down to

>	Genna's & run into
>	Robert at the bar.

He knows where I've been
His eyes are made of steel.

He says: "Tell my friend about the whale
that sunk that boat. She thinks
I'm crazy," and the blonde woman he's with
rolls her eyes and he tells me they're going
to be married and she says, "ha ha ha."

"Oh yeah," I said,
"The Sussex, that whaler that –"

"No, The Essex," he says.
"Explain to Ellen –"

"Yeah, explain it to me," she said.

Because you can't not not do it
and why not a whale and what
does anyone know about whales
who hasn't spent years
chasing them? and I don't
don't do it. Melville's man

who opened his heart
the slow drip of humanity

when the whale rammed the ship
twice & sent her down –
it wasn't, like, an *accident*.

The crew that survived floated about the Pacific
slowly dying of thirst, starvation,
and each other.
                    My tongue grew
thick. I looked around for the bartender.
Beauty, on a Pacific beach.

"If we turn the boat
to Tahiti, it's only a few days away."

"But there are cannibal tribes there."

So they resolved to sail across the Pacific
in those open boats
                    – at least we'll be safe
from the mercies of the native.
                    A civilized crew –
a handshake and steady eye and we're in this together.

The Essex, like Melville's Pequod,
was an integrated ship:
black and white, but only white men
climbed out of the lifeboat at journey's end.
Where are the black men, our mates, our crew?

Somewhere under the hard silence
of the equatorial sun,
the boat creaks homeward.

Why excite yourself over it? You may
as well join the circus and disabuse
small animals of their heads as attempt
to tell beauty anything about hunger.

If friendship is looking without consuming
the whale is our best friend –
circling round the men in their self-carnage,
she comes closer for a look.
She's thinking it over, wonders
at her own anger.

Before Melville wrote his whale book, he
visited the Essex' retired captain
at his home in Nantucket.

The old captain had put on weight. "Gravity,"
Melville called it. He'd turned his back
on the sea to take the job
of city nightwatchman.

Every night, the old cannibal
walked the streets, checking the locks
and doors of the wives, sons, and daughters
of the New England whalemen
as they slept. Constant slap &
saltwater splashing along the quay.
Tide coming in, the ocean a living thing
tugging at the boats and weeds
waving goodbye from the docks

and the conger eels of Cape Cod
leave the continental shelf
during the summer, cross
the Gulf Stream, and make

their way to the Sargasso Sea;
here they spawn in floating masses
of sargassum in the autumn and winter,
after which they are believed to die.

And the drinks arrived and we took a glass
or two in silence and Robert's friend put down
her glass at last and looking about saying:

"Ah, wine is good, and confidence is good;
but can wine or confidence percolate down
through all the pelagic strata
of hard consideration,
and flow warmly into cold benthic
truth?
        Truth will not be comforted.

Led by dear charity, lured by sweet hope,
fond fancy attempts it; but in vain; mere dreams
and ideals, they explode in your hand,
leaving nothing but the scorching behind."

We looked on her in surprise and she pass'd
her hand over her eyes saying, "sorry,
sorry. I've had too much." And Robert

only laugh'd, "why what's all this?
                    Here you
were left to your own and now you break out
like the Irish Rebellion 10,000 strong or the
Viet Minh all at once upon our cryptic hearts."

"I don't know," she replied. "I don't know what
it is. I must go, it's late and now there's nothing."

And with that she was gone and my brother
told me once how in Colorado he stopped
at a roadside attraction – semi trailer
by the highway "Winky the Whale"

in bright colors
on the side of the truck.
                    The creature
                    playing in
                    vivid scenes of ocean and sky
                    and seals and fishes.
                    And the cantankerous
                    old carny was on break
                    and didn't want to open up,
                    but for the couple of bucks
                    he pull'd wide the door
                    and in the dank, stale
                    cave of the semi
my brother approach'd
the whale, and
found the rotting
carcass of the creature
in a vat of formaldehyde
smelling of death & decay.
                    Our legacy writ
in poor attention to after the fact –
because Winky would
have sunk that
fucking Essex in a heartbeat.

ALAIN LESSONS

School days

Their fear of one-point perspective
~~Within the limits~~ kept them from approaching
the edges, such of course, is
what we call "heaven," ~~imposed by~~
~~destiny, the gods~~ though
here the food is served somewhat
~~highhandedly dispensed~~ warmer.
Do not erase – crossing out

is allowed, it leaves a trace of what ~~victory and ruin.~~
went before even if
even if ~~only~~ people are what
is meant. ~~They are always the ones~~
~~to provoke~~

      It turns out the essay
(following Alain's example) was written
first, then crossed out – leaving what
was legible – ~~which was of no importance~~
~~whatever other than~~ the letters'
curious attitude of regret and
~~betrayals that preclude peace;~~ bereavement
left alone there, the disaster ~~war is their~~
~~true métier, whim and~~ of meaning –
struck through all about them.

KNOT OF ACTION

*While still clinging to the architecture of the past, the
work now offers up the padding and voids that are the
architect's means of shaping space.*
    – DETROIT'S MICHIGAN THEATER

Thrown so far out of my body, electrical
cording, plaster dust, lathing, drifting haze of
asbestos in the air
                    (you'll die a millionaire).
                                    Do you find

people sacred as people or as individuals?

De Beauvoir admired her "ability to feel halfway
around the world." They met one day
on the playground.
                Simone (Weil)
                            declared in "no uncertain
terms" that only one thing mattered:
The revolution which would feed the starving.

Simone (dB) retorted that the problem
was not to make men happy,
but to find the reason for their existence:
"Are there men
            really?"

Weil (Simone) (and now everyone else)
looked her up and down: "it's clear
you've never gone hungry."

Gone hungry. Deny that you go hungry
as you motor about in your little boat
with Fidel & Jean Paul.
                    Years later
Weil plays Myrna Loy to Jesus' Thin Man:
                              "Did you
see that shady character skulking
around the arcade of 10,000 things?"
He asks, downing the martini of infinite wisdom.
Simone: "that was no character –
it was only some flâneur.

                    How many,
              excuse me, of those
have you had & can I
              get some?
        Oh Lord, you're leaking –"

"It's the stigmata acting up again," says Jesus "– mind the tablecloth."

                    knot of action

                            Tense
              and slack the line
              body & tools (industry itself) –
              geometrical concepts
              rendered material. Doubts
              doubt; all tied up for you
              in a ribbon of doubt –
              as in the scrutable
              arch of Wm. Powell's brow:
              collateral made flesh.
              Blind man's cue tapping
              the motive of the world.

EWIGKEIT

*We will not have a method for shaking off oppression
until the day when we have understood the causes of
oppression as clearly as we conceive the conditions of
the equilibrium of a stone.*
                                    – SIMONE WEIL

            equilibrium
of a stone.
Work
defined as lifting
        dead weight.

One stone
        falling,
rolling along the grassy
        bank into
the earth.

A small poison
    in your ear where you
        slept –
then into
grass thou hence did glide.

What does it mean
    to labor? There is no
consummation of theory
    & experience
when you're not to own land or
set up: dead weight and
knocked down as so many old
    stones in a graveyard.

MONDRIAN'S WHITES RECALLED

for being complex
and very fast. He built

them up gradually
layer on pasty layer.

A follower of Madam
Blavatsky, he needed

to get beyond a world
of forms where late-

Roman frescoes still
show the gods of

harvest: in winter &
spring the dance, but these

never depict the slaves
working the fields

bringing in the wealth, waiting
        upon the darker gods

that devour all the light –
all the color of the world.

ON MARX

The proletariat will produce its way
out of capitalism?
               How bourgeois.
Mr. Trotsky responded to her
criticism:
           Pity the fool
           who defends her personality
           against society.

Though T. took time out
from defending his own person
to drop in on Simone in Paris
and construct the Fourth International
in her parents' attic.

If the neighborhood bully
had only taken her bus money
she would have been spared
the Renault factory, the war
in Spain.
           But if the person is not
more interesting as an individual,
where else might we find
solace?

           Early one morning,
one morning in May, I spied
Pentheus at Aulis pursued by
a maiden or ten –

                    this just in
from our correspondent at Troy:
We're taking you live to the dust up
in the Dardanelles
with Horsebreaker Hector now on
our Actioncam, Wolf?

                    Yes, Hector
and the other children running the laps
'round the city, fleeing
the wild beasts set loose
from the Bourse, they're
well ahead thus far –
nothing to worry about –
                                unless
the currency collapse catches them up.

As Simone has it: the true subject of the
poem is force (not lamentation). Where else
will Ernst Jünger, stahlgewittert, ankle-deep
in Diomedes' trench,
                    find the
consolation of Israel, now personality
is a type of luxury?

                    Soldier, oh soldier,
I won't marry you,
            though you
bring a coat of
            leather and the
banker's head, too.

MANAGERIAL CLASS

> *Past revolutions had depended on the gradual previous*
> *establishment of a social and economic base from which*
> *to launch their revolutionary project, as the bourgeoisie*
> *had done in feudal society: the only group whose accession*
> *to power was being prepared in capitalist and socialist*
> *societies alike was the new managerial class of technicians.*
> – SIMONE WEIL

The archaeologist produces the stone,
some sort of poetic statement wrapped

in a wedding veil: "to prevent the work
from disintegrating into separate parts –

scattering sentence-rubble haphazard
on the waste heap." At the bottom

of the pyramid the bodies pile up
like tiny stromatolites.
                                    The
captives were stripped and hooded
with a certain residue of
reasonableness and set up
in secret policeman's tableaux.

Was this in the grant proposal? The
scientist gets it: Twenty-four hours

of Achy-Breaky Heart and resistance
crumbles. We sing their praise: Once

the cudgel & the prince's thug
to pull the tongue
and slit the throat; now
it's left to the clerk. He's left his card

at the door (all in good fun as they say,
a fraternal ritual): another

extraordinary rendition of an old tune
we'd flattered ourselves we didn't know.

SIMONE'S CIGARETTE BREAK

– Factory year

There was one disastrous incident
when she broke a tooth

in her industrial band saw while
daydreaming of Trotsky's youth and

his choice between Populism
and Marxism; but she went

home happy when she managed
to set up and recenter
the machine on her own.

Hand me a rivet, Anastasia. And what of the White Russians at work in the Renault Motor Works? They are dreaming of being Romanovs, or servants of Romanovs, as they smashed their rivets. The Renault factory built better tanks than the Germans, but they were deployed individually against groups of German tanks. Renault's factory girl, Simone Weil, settled on her industrial top while daydreaming of the ideological dilemmas of Trotsky's youth. No problem: She'd learned to re-focus the monsters herself, and the Renault tanks fired pure speculative bullets off the head of a small bourgeois German.

TWO

POST-HUMAN

Wm. James: the point
of being human
is to control one's own
attention.

PERSEPHONE'S BEES

Persephone's mother
was addressed as the
Pure Mother Bee.
She wept for her daughter
and the cottagers
gave her shelter – we know
the scene from
Frankenstein's Monster
taken in by the blind man.

Pure Mother Bee weeping
by the side of the road.
                In
exchange she taught them honey –
the anthropologist's
signifier of cultural transition
from the raw to the
cooked, and still used
throughout the Middle East
as preservative & smuggler's
cover for explosives. She
wept for her daughter
carried off before her
time. She wept by the side
of the road where the trucks
grind past all night without stopping.

FACTORY GIRL

Simone Weil skips lunch
in the cafeteria. The

carrots, too orange, the
Salisbury steak, too much

its own presence: no
sense of what it may

have been instead. She denies
the bread – nor will she

eat cake; jello only reminds
her of Nietzsche's final agony,

& the croque monsieur?
Please. And De Gaulle thought he'd

hire her to run the
new republic's schools.

WEIL AT WAR

After George Herbert

Simone, near-sighted
soldier of the Spanish

war, distracted
(the whisper of an inner

ear), foot hesitating
above the campfire's

cookpot (set in your
path deliberately by

Stalinists), no doubt in
that moment of insight

the heavens open'd and she
heard the sharp groan of

Henry Miller – bored with
all the whores of

Luxembourg. He dreams –
transports of

conversation with that girl
who took him for

several days – free. The
erotic love of

God looking, not
taking one step toward

the friend, but flying
upward. Sit & taste

Love, the meat served
the unrequited guest.

ON THE LAKE

This festival's over. The ferry docked
& we climbed up to the town. The streets
stained red with spilled wine,
winemakers in work boots trundled
the casks back to cellarage. The workmen
leveraging barrels won't look us
in the eye. There comes a time when
even delight reaches its limit and here
the closing of the harvest turns to
the click of bootheels on pavement.
We hear the clash and roll of empties
dispatched down stairwells.
                                              Couples
stagger against each other up the street.
A laughing group gathers 'round
a closed shop – unwilling to move on,
squeezing one more laugh from th'year's
harvest of embarrassment. Aficionados
argue that the region is unsurpassed –
but it could be anywhere: another
stumble of pursuer and the pursued.
We return to quayside watching the
water darken: daylight no longer
caught in this reflection. The trees bend
under the ripening green walnuts of fall.

CATHAR KINKS

The shepherds pursued their
animals back and forth over
the Pyrenees for generations –

almost a country in itself. The
Inquisition took its time,
waiting years for men to return

to Carcassonne from the south
to be arrested by the soldiers, &
questioned by the priests.
                              The
heretics had *parfaits*, their
holy men and women,
                              and in the end
these were reduced to refugees
in hiding from the Catholics.

                              Pierre
had hidden the holy man, for years,
listened to his preaching. "This world
was made by the Devil, thus, we
should not take pleasure in evil;
do not make children, or love; this only
brings pleasure
                    to the Enemy." And
Pierre returned home
once from the mountain to find
the music cranked up full volume:
The Kinks singing Waterloo
& the holy man in Pierre's bed lying
between his wife's legs

there
the holy man jumped up saying, "it's not
what it seems, my friend. My work
       here is only to observe
            these evils the demon
has set for you. I tell you, Pierre,
       your soul is in mortal danger and
the precipice is near at hand."

                              And Pierre
went away wishing they had
not been playing his
favorite song so loud that he would
never listen to that shimmer again
without thinking on the evils
of this world & his poor wife's fate in
such a place,
            but as he told
the holy man later as they ate their
evening meal
                  (that technically the priest
should not have enjoyed so well):
the singer of that rhyme may indeed
have been a parfait as well: he only
watches the pleasure of others,

            Terry meets Julie
            Waterloo Station
            every Friday night...
            sha la la...

crossing the river to Chelsea –

Ah, but some do not cross, do they brother?
but they make

                    their homes
                                    where they may.

"Just so, just so," replied the holy man.
"One observes the fruit of the tree
while another gobbles it up.
                                    Are you
using that last piece of bread?"
                                    And the
Inquisition took up the holy man that year
& burn'd him for his work.

INCOMMENSURABILITY

Incommensurability
not the tragedy
for Greek
thought...

wind out of Southeast,
proceeded laterally for
landfalle with no
torpedoes amidships
we ate
lobster tails making faces
at the mathematician clever
with the number 13

[Ritual murder is the
epitome
of the sacrificial aesthetic

    But (,)

freed from ethical responsibility.]

Surrey?

  tender pigeons flying first
  indignantly then
leg band reciprocal communication

Mars say '41

Nos vemos, Simone. Internment
let you slide
the rails –
Casablanca? No romance
there, you'd've painted
your face
(as you did once
in Paris passing as
the factory girl)
carrying
an explosive in your purse
to the discotheque.

Out for groceries, the posters
announce the open city:
the enemy inside
the gates.
O Aeneas, you fled south,
your parents
on your back,
the household gods
Oppression & liberty
left at the flat.

RADIUS

No dreams in isolation.

"Radicchio ha. Maybe alfalfa,"
the farmer said. "I've seen
you at the neighbor's walking
them beans."

        "The field
is open," she said. "And I
have studied the lines
of Avicenna, Herbert, and
Homer the divine."

"Don't know them. Sound
foreign, but the yellow
horse knows the way. The
rain of last evening will give
an easy row and slick."

She took the reins offer'd
and stood long in place,
the horse shudder'd,
fix'd on some further star.

        The
angel of history forever
retreating, looking back
in horror on the future she
creates.
     The nervous horse
catches a glimpse of the banker

behind the stun hammer
at the glue factory. "All fields
are sown as they always will be.
The future is no undiscover'd
country waiting upon our
astonish'd eyes.
            You have
fed us all ten thousand years,"
she said.
          "Maybe, but this
here's winter forage for –"

          And she gave
a loud shout and the horse
jump'd as though across
the sky, the plow a shamble
in joy and tangled mass of board,
broken armature, and leather.

The commissars
would have whipped her.

          The farmer chased
her from the field, cursing her –
broken the poet's smooth line.

FARM LABOR 1941

> *If there is something irreducible,*
> *it is that which has an infinite*
> *value.*
>
> – SIMONE WEIL

Farm labor (this is before
genetic engineering – not much
irreducible now the

tomatoes raised on a
crutch of salmon bones).
The end of a day
and necessity
burns off all
contingencies.

Where she finally
bisects the circle – the

infinite ray – all angles
formed right & the
world fell away; as though

the personality is a
sort of angle or deviation from
the straight angle of

divinity.
          When the snowfall
began and the German tanks
failed before Moscow,

the Vietnamese munitions
workers intern'd
in Marseilles were given

brooms to sweep snow
from the streets. They stood in
astonishment at the falling snow.

                    Indochina
had never shown them
such a thing, & they

would never see its like again –
                    except
one or two of these

pausing at a broom,
would remember such labor
years later when

they stood beside
the Red River of Vietnam,
watching the white

silk parachutes
of the French army
floating into distant valleys.

FILA M ENT O

Under the sign of filamento
in San Francisco, I traded words
with the RCP – Lyndon
LaRoucheniks they were, and
spooky as an embassy.

All the while the billboard
above our heads, horribly kern'd,
unreadable, and squat ugly.

Nothing we could say would
change that material dialectic:
that this famously upscale shop
would see fit to post its name
in six-foot letters that had
clearly never seen the touch
of anyone who knew their craft.

MRS. MCCORMACK'S CHILDREN

i.m. M. Marprelate

After Veblen
    again pointing
        to the fact
of our degenerate
    character, we printers
changing jobs
      and masters
           from city to city –
    rootless ones.

> *He would pour out some wine for me and some for himself – wine*
> *which tasted of the sun and of the soil upon which this city was*
> *built. At other times we would stretch ourselves out on the floor of*
> *the garret, and sweet sleep would enfold me. Then I would wake*
> *and drink in the light of the sun.*

Simone wakes again in the attic
    with Christ
      by her side, drinking
the light of the sun, etc:

    Thinking of her ex, Richard II,
who told her
    she was born
a serf and serf she would remain

    & in this romantic comedy
of one doom'd king or another
    Simone thrilled to hear this.

Let us trace the evolution,
Jesus, back through Bunyan
to the Interregnum pamphlets
of Levellers and Diggers
ultimately to
Puritan sermons
and Marprelate:

*Robert Waldegrave dares not shew his face for the
bloodthirsty desire you have for his life, only for printing
of books which touch the bishop's mitres. You know that
Waldegrave's printing press and letters were taken away.
His press, being timber, was sawn and hewed in pieces,
the ironwork battered and made unserviceable, his letters
melted, with cases and other tools defaced (by John
Woolfe, Beadle of the Stationers, and most tormenting
executioner of Waldegrave's goods), and he himself
utterly deprived forever of printing again, having a wife
and five small children. Will this monstrous cruelty
never be revenged, think you? When Waldegrave's goods
was to be spoiled and defaced there were some printers
that rather than all the goods should be spoiled offered
money for it, towards the relief of the man's wife and
children, but this could not be obtained...*

First   the plague
and after   the workmen

began to move from place
to place   ready to take

advantage   of   any

variation   in the
demand   for labor

in the   demand
of place   variation

of all the linotype workers –
two finger typists all –

none remain. The bare
bulb hangs above the

machine switched off and
our position gone dark.

Gerrard Winstanley (Digger) and Marprelate
Your digging does maintain, and persons all defame
Stand up now, stand up.

Your houses they pull down, stand up now
Stand up

And then afterward:
I have gone out into a future
that is mine without you.

Do not think I am
afraid of time, it is

the country
             of my
birth, now good
your grace, it is now
you know it as the
        relentless place
of loss,
        when there's
some excitement here
I note it down
for your return to
tell you, my love, of
the crushing heave of
        the world's breath,
I remember you now
your hair as you lay
your head on my chest all
dunsticall and absurd
        as we were.

||

this country seems so much
smaller now our position gone dark &

the kindness you showed me then
a burr under my tongue.

The gray November light
soft   across the attic ceiling
when you poured out some wine for

The architectural details
    you liked so much and which I intend
to proclaim in next decree

all lovers lie
in impossibility
of avoiding
or prettifying

November together
when we'd forgotten all day to rise

the absolute
practical expression of

        Witness,
                my Grace,
        the greater prevalence of dissipation
        among printers than among the average

        workmen – attributable
        to the greater ease in movement

        and the more transient character
        of acquaintance & human contact
        in this trade.

                Skill acquired in any
        printing house or any city is easily

        turned to account in almost any
        other house or city; that is to say

        the inertia due to special training
        is slight. Also, this occupation

requires
more than the average of intelligence
and general information, and those

employed in it
are therefore
ordinarily more ready than many

others to take advantage of any
slight
variation in the demand
for labor from one place to another.

||

The Young Irelanders took their inspiration
from the revolution in France (1848)
and chased a group of policemen into the Widow
McCormack's farmhouse.
                              Wm. O'Brien,
the leader, went up to the window to negotiate
& the policemen shot him.
                              A general
fusillade ensuing, the Widow demanding
of the wounded O'Brien:
"and what will happen to my five children –
hostages of the policemen?"
                              Absolutely
nothing, madam, the rebels being terrible
shots, though this being the second year of
famine, shooting them might be for the best.

||

And now good your grace,
the serfs are massing at Foxconn
and the King rides out to them:
"Serf you were born..."

[This poem written on Foxconn
tablet and read thereon my lord this year...]

the peasants demand
the right to move to take advantage
following Instanter on the slight changes
in labor market
               and Wat Tyler
nudges George Herbert who is
palmed in a pamphlet thereby
to Simone Weil in the ruined
cathedral of European humanism.

| |

MARX WRITES to the executive:
He's excited
   (in one of his moods)

     a little nervous, yes,
but the uprising in Paris
   is going well
     and word has it

Johnny Marr will soon appear
    with the Young
      Irelanders to play

those chiming guitar bits. Karl
    disappointed with the
        singing of the Mountain:

"the chest notes were missing,"
    as the Occupy protesters
        made their way along

the Boulevard calling for Change and
    the party of Order met them
        with chasseurs and dragoons

in an altogether unparliamentary way,
    driving the kerls before them.
        And Karl, for his part, has

found a young Frenchwoman living in exile
    in London and all
        she will talk about

is walking. The labor of taking
    one step forward
        and he wants to get

her on the printer's committee
    just one time.

> By walking, I mean, men's reversèd feet
> I chanced another world to meet;
>
> Another face presents below,
> Where people's feet against ours go.

| |

And there they caught Marprelate's printer
in London & had him eviscerated,
with the king's foot upon
rebellion's neck and even so poor
a son of Wat Tyler as Martin Marprelate
demanding:

When Adam delv'd and Eve span –

The sunrise over the Paris roofline
and the foot on the neck in 1848,
and again in 1870:

who was then the gentleman?

| |

He would pour out some
wine for me and some
for himself.

Then I would awake
and drink in the light

of the neon sign – no Chinese
walls to slow the penetration of the market

| |

In later years, Marx, sick
with catarrh, liver disease,

hemorrhoids,
          begins to suspect that Material
     Conditions have taken a
particular interest in him
     personally
               labor entering

into the body & indeed the kindness of
a pearl you left on my tongue and the

impossibility
of avoiding
     or prettifying

any longer the absolute
     imperative misery

and practical expression
     of love
entering into the body where

Marx then in the petty
bourgeois procession

of 1849 and the chest notes
weren't in it
               left to
                    chanting *vive l'amour*
and met by *chasseurs*. The streets –
whose streets? vacant and cleared.

News agents assaulted & (stand
up now) the students kettled for the
length of the day. Shops shuttered,
and the wind blows through me.

Material Conditions drunk texting
    Marx: lascivious notions of
        use value – completely nude

> *and you know that the Legion of High Finance on June
> 13 raided the print shops of Boulé and Roux, demolished
> the presses, arrested editors, compositors, printers, ship-
> ping clerks, and errand boys, the hacker who download-
> ed the emails given the longest sentence permitted by law
> handed down from my lord's Star Chamber.*

When we find ourselves
like Mrs. McCormack's five
young boys – survivors

in an emigrant prairie –
land of absence with the speculators'
mansions rising up, dark

watchtowers around us –
another place where I am you
cannot be. Not a place

but a variation in demand
carved up by speculation; mostly
Yankee transplants from the East
– toilets cleaned & kitchens staff'd
by the Irish and German.

And in all love I'm thinking:
    my people.

Notes:

p. 45. After Veblen again pointing... "The Theory of the Leisure Class" I was reading for tribal aesthetics, and Veblen's notes on consumption patterns are loaded with tribal code. Consumption and waste are signifiers of status and anxiety. cf: any office building's parking lot.

p. 45, He would pour out some wine ... Simone Weil.

p. 46, Robert Waldegrave dares not shew... Christopher Hill on the Diggers and dissenters of 17th century England.

p. 51, and the King rides out... The Peasants' Rebellion of 1381. Confluence of the 21st century and the Peasants' Rebellion of 1381 is the tension between labor's desire for freedom of movement while capital will have us stay in place. Richard II tells us: "serfs you are and serfs you shall remain." The Chinese (and possibly soon the Wisconsinites) who labor in the Foxconn plants tell us, "we're going to move."

p. 51, Wat Tyler nudges George Herbert... Tyler was a leader of the Peasant's Rebellion. Herbert a poet that Weil admired.

p. 52, "the chest notes were missing..." from Marx's journalism on the 1848 revolutions and the 1870 Paris Commune.

p. 55, Carved up by speculators... The History of Wisconsin Atlas. Irish and German settlement of Wisconsin following the 1848 debacles of the Young Irelanders/Famine and Köln rebellions.

THE OFFERING

Fall slope in ocean currents

       of air or water.

I don't know, a little east of the river

to the narrow road in the west,
the scraggly lot of them off the boat

and handed a grubstake: Five dollars
in the local currency. My great

grandmother standing
at dockside ready to
demonstrate that same sharp
financial savvy I've inherited,

tore the money in two: "I don't want
your durrty paper." Into the
drink it went – into the ocean
that had just released her.

      Look out, America,
she was here to set you straight
– another Jonah franchise
thrown up on the beach. Even if
you'd paved your streets
in the promised gold,
you'd never have cover'd
the costs coming due.

THREE

COMRADE ORLOV'S TIMESHARE

Alexander Mikhailovich Orlov (1895 – 1973) was a colonel in the Soviet secret police and NKVD Rezident in the Second Spanish Republic. In 1938, fearing execution, he went on the run, writing a letter to Stalin promising silence. He fled with his family to the United States where he lived quietly and undetected until the death of Stalin. Orlov died in Cleveland, Ohio, making his living as a Realtor.

Summer of Love and Papa's hands
blue-knuckled on the wheel.
Double line of smoke unspools

from the cigarette
on his lip.
        The daughter
cranks the window down
and follows her father's gaze
to the bookstore across
the street. She knows not
to speak.
        The old man
puts the car into gear
and off they go.

          He likes an
estate sale, a house showing,
        thinking on all those
Trots at the commie bookstore
in Coventry.
        His daughter,
10 years old, squirms in place,

and he looks at her
as if he didn't know her. "Joe,"
he says to himself, not
for the first time that day,
or the last, "Uncle Joe,
you'll never hear a peep
outa me, like they say here
in the gangster flicks:
                              not a

                                   peep.
I promise you." He learned
his way around the exciting
give & take of American
Real Estate – help the boys
coming home from the war
to find a home –
                         Murphy's
all right, even Bronsky,
and nothin' but
nothin' for Washington.

Of Cleveland's winters, snow
& north wind off the lake –
meh, they call
      this winter? Though
he dreams of winter's banyas.

The summer stench of Cuyahoga;
      the dead air of the Flats –
and the money splashed
      across the escarpments
ringing the city.
                         The time
parked by the hippy
bookstore never seem'd long

to Orlov. Love beads and rosy
round glasses.
                      The past plays and
spatters in the mind.
Maybe if he could pull one
    aside & say, "look –"
but don't let's talk of Spain now.

Beach life and condos
    cover a world
of sins. It's back to work and
    Orlov sweats the closing.

He decides to play it Major Strasser
for a quiet laugh. Conrad Voigt –
there was a mensch – *Waxworks*,
Orlov's favorite film. Voigt as

Ivan the Terrible – poisoning
all Russia. He plays it up:
uncapping the fountain pen,
holding the man's gaze,

a long breath before sliding
it slow across
the table, thinking
    on all you know, all
the confessions extracted
& signed – just like this.

                    And in America,
they leave you keep your fingernails.
The buyer grabs the pen. He's
eager to do it. They all come round
eventually. Oh, Joe, what
you could've done in a place like this.

DEFINE THIS WORD

> *That early spring I met a young servant in northern*
> *Burgundy who was almost fanatical about food, like a*
> *medieval woman possessed by the devil. Her obsession*
> *engulfed even my appreciation of the dishes she served,*
> *until I grew uncomfortable.*
> — M.F.K. FISHER, 'DEFINE THIS WORD'

1

In France, Fisher conquers
the menu. But when the obsessive
young woman brings the trout
gleaming in its bucket of water
she misses the reference to
Cuchulain and the trout that waits
at the bottom of the pool,
the secret in its mouth.

If Simone's factory year
had been in the service industry
rather than the production line:
Gateaux, instead of gaskets, she'd've
served it up by the shovelful –
gladly taken up the knife,
explaining that any trout
(gleaming is of course better),
Madame Fisher, or Kennedy, or
whatever it is you call yourself –
but any trout is glad, truly glad
to suffer the infinite regression of my
knife of geometrical precision.

2

The knight pulls up
to the drive-through, his
battle-axe over his shoulder
like a bass guitar. Don't
meditate on the blood
of the trout, love, it's London
calling and De Gaulle in exile
wants to make Simone the
minister for education – a sop
to the Trots – but she would rather
a parachute battalion and a
nurse's kit.
                [The wounded Resistance
fighter looks into the sky
to see Simone Weil floating, floating
sister morphine to earth.]

                            But she
falls ill in London without portfolio,
no squad of nurses, she hasn't a silk
to carry her home.

3

Only the romantic would call it
starvation. Even here in London
          (it may have been the marmite
after all) there were buckets of trout,
but not the one she wanted –
that one
          [rising from the pool
(or Spanish cook pot) to whisper
in her ear]

                 lingers still,
piloting an airship far above
the ceiling height of human flyers –
fish goggles agleam
and chinstrap dangling loose.

                           Oh, go tell it
to Gawain. The old dirigible sinks
into a cloudbank, troutsong
echoing in the breeze.

SOMEWHERE SENSIBLE

The summoning from th' trees
like roses fading to unlike

enclosed in wire strung
someone sensible of

Christ's younger brother, Poseidon,
Compell'd with love & whisper'd

into plastic for
going, when man stopped short

spitting newly coined
usages found once stuttering

here, not a confession
bowered in her hair

unfolding some map first.
Fractured hymns so:

"love," I said. As though
my body turning

slipped parenthetically
between your hands.

RELATIVITY

1

working along the highway
the overgrown path

we lose the way in
Isaiah foretelling

the light already in motion
toward us.

Certainty in physics:
Dante watches the two

wretches playing table
tennis on the train moving

through a neighborhood of
hell, yet the little white

ball refuses to move – light
years of brooding ahead.

2

Morning when the details
of seeing collapse.

Matter never had it so easy,
the inventor

in frustration
retreats to cement

factory. He sulks
ten years, blowing

rocks to gravel with
dynamite. Repugnant

flat world –
light it up. Move

that mountain. His
genius would

shatter stone opens
only surface.

3
Reading the Synoptic
Mary refuses the

angel at the cave where
they'd laid Jesus' body

– the sepulcher. She demands
to see the body: 'Produce –

Produce the corpse,
motherfucker,' she says &

the angel throws down
on her and grapples her.

Our worser angels
cheat when at wrestling

but she breaks
his hold (the angel's only

one angel against Magdalene
– *the* Magdalene). She

rushes into the cave, calling
"help me, help me, Jesus,"

but the grave is empty,
but for the rustle of her breath.

NOTEBOOK COVERS

*I cannot conceive the necessity for God to love me, when
I feel so clearly that even with human beings affection for
me can only be a mistake. But I can easily imagine that He
loves that perception of creation which can only be seen from
the point where I am. But I act as a screen, I must withdraw
so that He may see it.*

         – SIMONE WEIL

All at once sinking into the luxuries
of proletarian revolution & the honesty

of the working man – it makes a pillow
for a young Pascal with bits of broken glass

where it don't fit. The colors
of the universe average out to the

gray-green tegument
discovered
       by Pythian Apollo's
                astronauts
seeking loose change behind the
cushions of the moon. If He loves

the perspective so much, tell Him
to get His Ass off the couch & get His own beer –

Something moves toward us
through the forest of equations,

a rustle behind the banyan
of Sanskrit, beneath

the covers of notebooks' scribbled
arcana – a child's tale: A youth

buttonholed by the crone
on the way to a wedding, whispered

in one's ear, after the habit of
hunger – *grabugeument* – teeth bared
snarling white emptiness behind you.

SURELY YOU SEE THAT

After Brecht

you'll go down –
　　　how do I
　　　know if you
　　　don't

speak up for yourself?
Crystal prisms caught mid-air
in morning light drifting 'cross brick
smokestacks & boarded
storefronts. Acetylene sparks &
　　　flying snow: hazy
indiscretions and downtown
constructions of the closing year.

HAUL OF THE MOUNTAIN KING

(The Immortal 3/4)

"What is the friend?" Simone asks. "Two
birds kissing in the tree?" Impatient
with Pythagoras, she sees the

rebuke in his answer: Our numbers | rarely add up friendly –
(Or that someone could conceive an affection for me).

"The friend is the other I." "M" is for master –
the killer of innocents – describing
his flight from his shadow,

Peter Lorre: "Ich will weg..." | But there's no exit strategy;

the bird continues eating and all the adepts die
in the mountains of cyanide.
M, tell us then, what is a friend?

He almost convinces, but when he says it again
in French, no one believes him. (It was
only a mix up at the crossing over,

who would pursue us outside of our own tongue?)
That transhumance

over the Pyrenees paused
at the border; Siegfried, Albert,
and Walter – they lean against each
other, stumbling along. By the gnosis

of his gnomon the pilgrim triangulates the distance
from his mountain to the ship passing
(whistling in descending thirds)

down the Catalan shore to Algiers. Here,
                                    the guidebooks all say, you'll

find the similarity of triangles
with all your sides alike. And there,
where we stumbled from our Arcadia,
the companion fell headlong from the roof.

Whom the gods would destroy, they first make
stutterers. The distance to the ship
carrying Simone into exile remains

proportional to the angle of Byzantium – where a gyring
of mimesis takes shape in the smoke
belching from those steamers
clearing the horizon.

SIMONE AT GOLF

Like a flower waiting to bloom,
Like a light bulb in a dark room,
I'm here waiting for you
to come on home and turn me on.
— NINA SIMONE

He would
pour out some wine for me
and some for himself
— wine
which tasted of the sun
and the soil upon which
this city was built.

We stretch out upon the floor
of the garret, until sweet
sleep enfolds me.
I wake to drink
the light of the sun.

A keening
ghost along the road, rough stone
pleated under knee.
Simone
Weil in New York is no Trotsky —
dropping in on the movie sets
of Babylon. She barely
goes out at all — it was the
season when Breton released
his attack butterflies on
Manhattan.

What could America give her?
                          She
writes the story of the stranger
who takes her to his room, but
she misses Hart's view
of the bridge. Instead, she
& her boyfriend watch
the traffick
                (Terry and Julie
cross over the river)
                        bending
the geometrical bow
of bread and wine, type
and topology, counter & spur.

Travelers of the city's Lachrymal
Terminal, they taste the sun & soil
upon which her city was built –
    not Hart's infinite ray

across her increasingly tangential
future, but they dream again
the rooftops of Paris,
and memory of Commune.

                          She
finds no ragged Algren here
for a picnic on Union Pier,
but on the day de Beauvoir &
Weil go golfing in Little Neck,
Simone Weil shuffles along
unsteady under the wasting
that will carry her off.

She addresses the ball

and smacks it high, straight
through the contradiction
        of the One
(which is not a number,
therefore,
        & yet).

                And the
white orb flies
                completely outasight

        carried on the wings
        of the little tailor
        (union local 1320) –
        & de Beauvoir gets it,
        she drops her little stick
        of the golf and, finally,
        learns to piss standing up.

SECOND SHIFT

After Ovid

       Slat bench in a basement.
    Workcrews not yet fixed. We wait
        for the manager to appear

   and count us off in fours
       for the daily
   twenty-story sweep of the building.

Wheeled bins to every crew
fitted out with cleansers & rags;

    two industrial-strength vacuums –
      women to the dusters,
    men to the vacuums.

Talking with Nguyen. He
had been a soldier. The

ARVN. "I was a lieutenant, now
American."
       And with that
he lifts his shirt showing

three bullet scars stitched
across his belly.
       In the fluorescent
light of the basement hallway

the scars blossom purple
tissue – blistered like
candy. You could almost peel them
from his skin – the scar tissue so bright –
and pop them in your mouth – savor of
cool morning in Dalat, or the
day they came down the Pleiku road

in armored columns the fear rising
in your throat –

       And there came a time
when helicopters didn't crowd the sky, when
bombers didn't come to hold you safe; nothing
between you and the high velocity air –

                               cover yourself,
the manager's coming. And away we go,
matador, floors assigned, vacuums and bins
parceled out;
         the squads go in fours
to elevator cars and up.
              Twenty years on:
each floor of the Mutual Insurance Company
swept clean by Nguyen – once chased
by Apollo, bag of dust filling as he went.

NIGHT BLESSING: A METAPHYSIC

*Simone Weil organizes her battalion of parachute nurses
for the drop into wartime France.*

*Il était Roparant, et le Vliqueux tarands
Allaient en gibroyant et en brimbulkdriquant
Jusque-là où la rourghe est à rouarghe à ramgmbde et
rangmbde à rouarghambde:
Tous les falomitards étaient les chats-huants
Et las Ghoré Uk'hatis dans le Grabugeument.*

         – "JABBERWOCKY," TRANSLATED BY ANTONIN ARTAUDI

It is a mistake to kill the Jabberwocky –
    Hemingway would have shot a million,
but they are hydra-headed, the Cerberus
    swamp beast emblem of geometric
progression. He wandered in the wood
    and shot himself in confusion at last.

Perhaps you came across dear Lawrence
    There in the blank labyrinth of sand. Did you
relieve him of his afflictions? Strike him
    hard as he required in all mercy in all
love? Or did you stay your hand:

        I have not
            made anyone weep –
        I have not made
            anyone afraid...

He went in tears from your kindness
and as if you loved me.

Maybe Stein would have bought your
    family's house – you were in flight in any case:
        "And one does not use nouns here
          and therefore slowly
        if you feel what is inside
          that thing you do not call it
        by the name which it is known."

II

This Night's blessing is the same joy only of
    pain. God presses our hand
close-crushing where I might once have said
    "yes." The root of cruelty is given us
a metaphysic: taken through the skin as

inconsolable mercy presses loss
    on us. For instance, crouch
as you will by the door with
    words of joy, overcome and
speechless with seeing you again
    after long absence – in light we are
disclosed, but enough or too much
and less of nothing is all we have.

Hyperbaton

The hospital levels off ecstatic
    overhead at five thousand feet.
                        A million
nurses floating a morphine fog into France
    can't staunch the blood.
                 Joan of Arc

presses hands of wounded soldiers
    jaws shot away, Homer's casque of

shattered brain and tongue meat
    pulp in balance of force [what is the

balance of force?]. We press
    harder. Know you're bless'd unspeakable
mercy now has your tongue a sweet kiss
    our father art naked in doorway

crouching – unable to make the bath, the city
    benchsleepers drop off so; the world hovers
above us: bread, wine, & opening flesh where
    your gentle fingers once spread the wound.

TWO YOUNG PIGEONS (SNOWFALL ON VICHY)

...and to offer in sacrifice / in keeping with what is said in the Law of the Lord: / "a pair of doves or two young pigeons."

Now there was a man / in Jerusalem called Simeon,
who was righteous and devout.
He was waiting for the consolation
of Israel, and the Holy Spirit was upon him.
— LUKE 2:24-25

Waiting for embarkation (or
some type of consolation) Simone
passes her days running messages
for the Resistance, writing
for Cahiers du Sud, and haunting
the Marseilles Cathedral.

Augustine dogs her steps
insisting the Church is
indeed these four walls,
the city: these twelve gates
(and so on). She turns and
walks, turns and walks, refusing
    the deal – and the mob never forgives her.

She says no, as Eugene
Debs says it. She says no, how
do you eat when
others are denied? If the feast
is set, better to crawl hand
and foot through the elegant
platters; like Maya Deren

escaping the cutting room floor,
dragging her feet through
the canapés. Let's say
it's set before you in easy,
microwave heaven, a little
Vichy sinecure in Clermont-Ferrand?
(I was not that Jewish – really.)

Would you take it? What
if it saves the others? [Don't worry,
they'll think of that as well.]

She turns and walks, turns
and walks to the open door, the
daylight only gray now – snow
falls on the city of
Marseilles.

           She leaves
as Czeslaw was coming in
(at that time we only knew
him as 'Elvis').
                 She pauses
at the doorstep: Snow falls
on the city,
           on German
agents & their refugees,
those with exit visas
and those without.
                   It drifts
into corners, swirls about
the streets and forms up in waves
pushed by the wind.
                   She
watches the Vietnamese

internees in their thin
blue smocks standing
in the gutters and along
the road scratching at the
snowfall with brooms. Soon,
they believe, they will be dismissed
and sent home in peace.

REFILL, HUN?

"They finally staunched the hemorrhage with
two long plastic tubes inserted into his nose
and inflated..." I hung up the phone, making

my excuses. Went to laundry, then breakfast
at the Greek place. Wondering about the
Peloponnese that they so learned their way

about an egg. Reading another Vallejo
poem – awaiting a death of mystery and
the inexplicable opacity of a flesh-eating
bacteria at work in the lungs until one is made

to feel a sensation of drowning, irrefutably
figured as the waiter arriving now with the urns
of her sacred office – turning the bright oval of this
dark cup blacker, the shade once of the old man's eye.

CHISHOLM GOODNIGHT LOVING

i.m. Ed Dorn

I

Showing up to class
early I found my poet
leaning over the
refuse bin set beside
the sidewalk, inspecting
the glitter of the pebbled lid.

"Oh, hey," he said. "Have
you ever looked at these
garbage cans before? I mean,
really looked – the
little stones here
sparkle so."
   No. No, I
never noticed. I believe
the whole thing's
coated in urethane.
 "Why do you suppose,"
he said, "we put our trash
in such bright things?"

II

He was not a real
cowboy. He had been
a bookkeeper in St. Paul
and he came out
to Montana for his health.

He had a bad
tuberculosis, and
after a few months
he got so sick
the old man brought
him into town and
left him. He said to
the rest of us: One
of you ought to stay.

He looked right at me
and I said I would stay.
The boy kept hemorrhaging
all over everything and
I took newspapers and spread
them out on the floor and on
the bedclothes.
He did not want me
to leave him for a minute.

III

I was a guest at Nestor's Hall when
Telemachus came looking for his father.

The old man sat the boy down, told him
stories of the War, Odysseus' parting

by the shore. We rolled the joint and
passed it, listening to the old man

talking about himself. He liked nothing
better. After some time, he stopped and fixed

the boy with a look. "Your sister –
don't you have a sister?"

IV

Marion Morrison in 3-D rides
upon his lone prairie. Git-along Daniel
Water'dstock Drew – Herman Confidence

Melville is a-crying out in the wilderness
for his children. A visionary: Daniel
Boone or mad bomber. The stock out of Texas

were immune to tick-borne disease, and
when the cattle drives rolled into
Kansas all the imported Hereford

of the locals up and died a yi yi. Rail- (and other)
heads shifted west – away from contagions
of settlement: Loving, Goodnight, Chisholm,

geologic time an accumulation of
paranoia (Dodge, Hays, Abilene;
every extension of the line pushing

John's face – he weren't a real
cowboy – up against the native's –
as if one had a choice).

V

I had been there with the kid
a week. Mr. Fuller came down one night
and he told me
you'd better go to bed. I hadn't

been to bed all that time,
only slept in a chair
once in a while, because he

wouldn't sleep unless he could lay
his head on my arm. So I
went and laid down in another
room. About midnight
Mr. Fuller come for me. "You'd

better come now. He's
asking for you."
                    I guess he knew
he was going. So I went
back where he was, and he

wanted to know if I would
lay down beside him and let
him rest his head on my
shoulder. In a few minutes

he mumbled something about
Ethel, his sister I think, and then
he was gone. I went off to
a honky-tonk first damn thing –

VI
Ethel, his sister, though
maybe he meant
Ethelred, the Saxon King
who married a
Norman princess and
opened the door
to William – that boy
was always talking
like that and we were
going to miss him
that winter no doubt.

Not a real cowboy, he
kept saying the
cattle drove us – not
the other way 'round.

VII

The shade of young
Elpenor loitered at the
end of the bar, coming
forward as the drink
was poured, resting
his shadow across my
arm as I drank.
                    "I was
a bookkeeper from St. Paul,"
he said. "Who was I
to sing all night
to the beasts? When I
was young I climbed
the roof of my parents'
house. I played in the
graveyard across the street from
where they'd buried that
Tom Horn. He's one
who outlived his time
and shot the wrong boy.

Or maybe it wasn't a
mistake. You can ask
him yourself – when he
comes up for a drink.

He kept a cabin in
Montana that the FBI
dismantled and presented
as evidence in Sacramento.

I have a sister, tell
her not to marry Canute,
the Dane. Make my
headstone of granite, flecked
            with mica –
let it shine under your sun."

CHRONOLOGY OF SIMONE WEIL

1909	Birth of Simone Weil
	Schooling in Paris
1931	Passes agrégation, thesis on Science and Perception in Descartes
	Begins teaching career in Le Puy
	Involvement in demonstrations of the unemployed
1932	Trade-union journalist
	Six weeks stay in Berlin
	Teaching in Auxerre
1933	Teaching in Rouanne
	Meets Trotsky
1934	Writes Oppression and Liberty
	Begins factory work in Paris
1935	Factory work
	Aug./Sept. Holiday in Spain
	Oct. Teaching at Bourges
1936	Fall. Joins anarchist militia in Spain
1937	Spring. Teaching in Saint Quentin
	Writes The Workers' Condition
1938	Summer. Travel in Italy
	Nov. First mystical experience
1939	Renounces pacifism in Cold War Policy in 1939
	Writes The Iliad: Poem of Force
	Drafts proposal for front line nurses
1940	Weils leave Paris, arrive in Marseilles after France falls to German
1941	Farm labor in Southern France
	Writing for the Caheirs du Sud
	Meets Perrin
1942	May. Leaves for America, via Casablanca
	July. Arrives in New York
	Dec. Travel to London.
1943	Work with De Gaulle's Free French government in exile
	July. Resign from Free French
	17 August. Enters Grosvenor Sanatorium, Ashford
	24 August. Death of Simone Weil

ABOUT THE AUTHOR

Kevin Ducey's short stories, essays, and poetry have appeared in Exquisite Corpse, AGNI, Crazyhorse, Beloit Poetry Journal, Stand, The Pinch, Notre Dame Review, and other places. His first book of poems, Rhinoceros, won the American Poetry Review's Honickman Award and was published by Copper Canyon Press. Cannot Exist, a press in Madison Wisconsin, published a chapbook of Ducey's translationsof Dante's Inferno.

Ducey has won writing awards and grants from the Wisconsin Arts Board, the Associated Writing Program, the Puffin Foundation, the Higgins Labor Foundation, Sonora Review, Booth Journal, and other places. He graduated with an MFA (in writing) from the University of Notre Dame in 2004, where he worked with John Matthias. He studied English, history, and film as an undergraduate at the University of Colorado at Boulder with Edward Dorn, Peter Michelson, and Gerda Norvig.

Ducey has made his living in a variety of fields including graphic design, editing, teaching (writing, ESL, and graphics), radio production, journalism, and food service, while not exactly earning a living as a musician, filmmaker, and performance artist. He has lived in Madison, San Francisco, Basel, Xalapa, Denver, Seoul, Cambridge, and Boulder. He currently lives in La Crosse, Wisconsin with the writer b.c. brown.

ABOUT KINGSTON UNIVERSITY PRESS

Kingston University Press has been publishing high-quality commercial and academic titles since 2009. Our list has always reflected the diverse nature of the student and academic bodies at the university in ways that are designed to impact on debate, to hear new voices, to generate mutual understanding, and to complement the values to which the university is committed.

While keeping true to our original mission, and maintaining our wide-ranging backlist titles, our most recent publishing focuses on bringing to the fore voices past and present that reflect and appeal to our community at the university as well as the wider reading community of readers, and writers in Kingston, the UK and beyond.

As well as publishing the work of writers and poets from the university's vibrant writing community, we also partner with other disciplines around the university, and organizations from our local community, to bring their content to a wider readership, and publish our own editions of older works.

Our books are all edited, designed and produced by students on Kingston University's MA and BA Publishing courses, whose creativity and publishing skills bring the projects to life.

Follow us on Twitter @KU_press and Instagram @kingstonuniversitypress